Ruminations at Twilight

Poetry Exploring the Sacred

Ruminations at Twilight

Poetry Exploring the Sacred

L.M. Browning

HOMEBOUND
PUBLICATIONS
Independent Publisher of Contemplative Titles

SECOND EDITION PUBLISHED BY HOMEBOUND PUBLICATIONS

Copyright © 2010, 2012 by L.M. Browning
All Rights Reserved

Without limiting the rights under copyright reserved above, no part of this publication may be reproduced, stored in or introduced into a retrieval system or transmitted in any means (electronic, mechanical, photocopying, recording or otherwise) without the prior written permission of both the copyright owner and publisher. Except for brief quotations embodied in critical articles and reviews.

For information or permissions write:
Homebound Publications,
PO Box 1442 Pawcatuck, Connecticut 06379-1968

SECOND EDITION
ISBN: 978-1-938846-04-5 (pbk)

First Edition published by
Little Red Tree Publishing 2010

VISIT HOMEBOUND PUBLICATIONS: WWW.HOMEBOUNDPUBLICATIONS.COM
VISIT THE AUTHOR AT: WWW.LMBROWNING.COM

BOOK DESIGN

Front Cover Image: Joshua Tree © Herman Layos | All Rights Reserved
Interior Image: © Robert Adrian Hillman | (Shuttershock.com)
Cover and Interior Design: Leslie M. Browning

Library of Congress Cataloging-in-Publication Data

Browning, L. M.
  Ruminations at twilight : poetry exploring the sacred / L.M. Browning. -- 2nd ed.
     p. cm.
  ISBN 978-1-938846-04-5 (pbk.)
  1. Spirituality--Poetry. I. Title.
  PS3602.R738R86 2012
  811'.6--dc23
                                                                    2012036062

10 9 8 7 6 5 4 3 2

ALSO BY L.M. BROWNING

POETRY

Oak Wise: Poetry Exploring an Ecological Faith
The Barren Plain: Poetry Exploring the Reality of the Modern Wasteland
Fleeting Moments of Fierce Clarity: Journal of a New England Poet

FICTION

The Nameless Man

Foreword

by J.K. McDowell

The poetry before you testifies to our twenty-first century spiritual existence. Ruminations are the much needed, deep reflections on where we are, where we have been and where we are going. The twilight is a setting of the betwixt and between. In twilight, a sideways sight is needed for proper navigation, proper witnessing and sighting a way forward, a way home. In *Ruminations at Twilight* L. M. Browning calls us to this important labor, at this important junction. We need to be in these spiritual waters, following the flows, marking the sorrows of progress, understanding the trespass of the modern. We need to be straining our eyes and our hearts to the limits needed to find the soul of our future, our true soul.

Ruminations at Twilight is a collection of ten poems that form a narrative of spiritual discovery. The poems should be read in order at least once. After that initiatory experience, the reader can revisit passages as a tonic of further reflection. The favorite phrases might serve as nourishment in times of unintended spiritual scarcity. Any troubling passages can serve as a penetrating balm, apply as much is needed to work through a particular or recurring soreness of spirit. The poetry here is for healing.

All readers will have their best-loved phrases, I am no different. I do have the privilege of sharing a few of my own favorites in this Foreword. There are many, here are just a few:

"You have made it so the river of your consciousness
flows through our very heart."

Browning is linking the sacred in the author and the sacred in the reader and both to the divine's design and intentions. This creates an important foundation and grounding for the reading ahead and the work after.

"To rediscover the lost world
     we must see the old with new eyes."

New and powerful senses are needed on this quest and with that a deepened understanding. I know Browning's roots are New England, yet in these words I hear the charge and call of William Blake.

"I walk through the stillness
searching for a divide
in the invisible cloth draped between us,
     that I might draw back the curtain
and enter the world in which you dwell."

And here the echoes of Irish Mystics, Yeats & A.E. The sacred is so close and yet unseen. The sacred is a treasure we once held and must now seek again.

"… I emerge with wings strong enough to carry me
beyond the desolation …"

For me, Browning becomes like a mythic Firebird, red, radiant, resplendent. The power of her poetry allows us an escape from danger and yet we have more work to do before we are whole.

"All I can offer are the sacred parts of myself:
    my heart, my lifetime,
    my body and my promise."

This confession is profound, this sacrifice honest, and the reader is motivated to do the same.

And the more troubling passages for me, I will keep private. We all have a fair amount of soul work to do. I will confess that *Ruminations at Twilight* presents a singular challenge to our times, where we are so immersed in technology. How does the passenger in seat 12C revisit the ancient, the natural, to recapture the sacred, while swiping a fingertip across the glass screen, to turn the page of the poem? I glance away from the backlit LCD screen and wonder at the clouds out the window. We need powerful "new eyes" and the vigilance to use them and share the miracles we see.

To discover or rediscover a work in its intended form, free of the intentions of others, is precious. This second edition of *Ruminations at Twilight* is such a treasure: ancient, updated to its original form, more than ever a beacon of hope and a challenge. If you have graced me with your eyes by reading this Foreword, please join me, honor the sacred in the ordinary. Drink with me at this well, these waters, so fresh, renew our hearts, and savor these *Ruminations at Twilight*.

Table of Contents

Foreword by J.K. McDowell ♦ vii

The Sacred ♦ 1

Coming Home ♦ 23

Inherent Knowledge ♦ 43

After the Night, Before the Day ♦ 63

The Language of the Mute ♦ 71

Original Form ♦ 81

The Two Sides ♦ 87

My Return to the New England Wood ♦ 101

Reentering the Womb ♦ 113

Hiraeth ♦ 119

About the Author

About the Publisher

The Sacred

You placed yourself in all that you created.
You live within the majesty of the world we uproot.
   …In the mountains we hollow out.
   …In the rushing rivers we dam.
   …In the old wood forests we burned.
   …In the graceful beasts we hunt to extinction.
   …In the soul you gave us,
      Which we were so eager to reshape.

We destroy you
Then damn you for forsaking us.

We hide you
Then demand to know
Why you have made yourself elusive.

We renounce you
Then accuse you
Of turning your back on us.

We left behind the simple ways
    —Disconnecting ourselves from
    What it is to be human—
Only to drive ourselves mad
Unable to answer the question: *Who am I?*

Always demanding more of you we say, "Speak!"
You shout to us with all your might,
Across the divide between
   Our disbelief
           And your endurance,
Coming to us only as a faint whisper.

Left deaf within our modern din
And dulled by our forgetfulness
We say: "Not enough. —Appear."

You come unto us in your shapeless form
   —A being woven from the fibers of spirit
   Invisible to the doubting eye,
   Luminous to the believing—
And, only seeing a vague shadow of you,
We dismiss you as a figment of our own longing.

You ever-dwell within and around;

While we are ever-asking when you shall appear.
You have made it so the river of your consciousness
Flows through our very heart.
Yet we feel that we have been neglected
And left to wander without tether or guide.

We have sought you out for millenniums on end,
              You—oh power beyond us.
Yet this next generation,
Who shall harness the genome,
Will leave behind their need for you;
For one does not feel the need
To seek out the greater power
If one perceives themselves to be greater still.

One will not seek out the deeper workings
If one presumes to already understand them.

One will not beg
For a miracle from a god
If one believes they can simply pay another man
              To be their savior.

The god of the ancestors will be left behind
As man finally assumes the role himself.
And I am left wondering if,
After the mobs who carved the idols of you disperse
—If after they put down the gilded images of you—
    Will those of us who stay,
        Finally come to see your true face?

If, once the mobs stop force-feeding
    All peoples the confining doctrine,
Might we not at last be able to hear your actual words?

If after the doors are closed on the theatrical mass,
Will those of us who still long to find you
Once again feel that pull to return to the ancient wood
Or stand upon the shore's edge where man's spirituality began
And find you there, in those places
Where the veil between worlds is thin?

As the frenzy and fanaticism dies,
    Religion is left behind
And the new age of man's own perceived omnipotence begins,
Will those of us who choose not to follow
Finally go back to our roots?

While the others begin the pending descent
Will we who remain go into the past to secure a future?

I know I will.

For I know that what we need to be complete,
Is not something that we can *invent*
But rather is something we must *resurrect*.
…It is not something that must be discovered,
                         But rather rediscovered.

We shall not be able to heal
The ailing soul with synthetics.
Therefore,
     No matter the medicines made to
Treat the symptoms of the body,
Humanity shall continue to decline.

Yet we need not fear.
What we need to heal ourselves still endures.
It flourished once before, in the eras past
     —Before the great books were written
     And the robes of priesthood were woven—
When it was simply man and woman
        And the other who dwelt beyond but near.

The savage in fur and buckskin,
Who had naught but his fire
And his tools made of bone,
Was wise enough to see
The sacredness of the world around him.

He recognized the magic
That lie in the movement of stars and planets,
In the ebb and flow of the tide,
In the waxing and waning of the moon,
In the miracle of the emerging seed
And the nourishing bounty to follow.

Yet the first thing we did
To try to establish our modern intelligence
Was to explain your magic as science.

We declared your wonders
        To be ordinary.
We took away your power
And gave it to the molecules of matter and energy.
We drained the fathomless ocean of the unknown
        And founded the shallow world.

We dismissed the cave-dweller
Who awed at the stars as simple-minded.
We declared the great mystery solved.
We emptied ourselves of belief,
And now we despair at the hollowness of life.

However, I can go no further.
I can follow no more the misguided.

I must part from the others
And go back to the place where we left you.
I am coming home to light the cold hearth.
I am coming home to till the overgrown fields.
I am coming home to you;
    Where I shall ask you, oh ancient one
     —Mother and father to all creatures—
        To take me back in.

We made you a god.
We gave you the throne and crown
In our attempt to understand
What it is to be all-powerful.
We likened you to a lord of men
    —A ruler with free reign—
For such was our idea of the omnipotent being.

However, you were never that, were you.

We imagined you in domed halls of marble,
The silver bearded judge and monarch—
    Commander of angels,
    Mover of worlds,
    Weaver of souls.
But that was never where you were.
…That was never what you were.

Our feeble minds,
Which held such wrong ideas of power,
Could never comprehend what you truly are.

Yes, oh primordial power, you exist
But we have not the eyes to see you.

You—the force from which we sprung—
Are a being that we cannot fathom.

It is not your absence
That keeps us from seeing you,
It is our own blindness.

You are there,
We simply have not
The awareness to recognize you.

Throughout our existence we have sought you,
All the while thinking you to be one person,
When in fact you are another.

And in our vain attempts to define you
We have only maimed you.
In our efforts to bring ourselves closer to you,
We have only brought ourselves farther away.

Now we are faced, not only with opening our minds
       But also with clearing them;
For we cannot come to understand what you truly are,
Until we find a way to let go of the past forms we gave to you.

I shall mourn the myth that dies;
Nevertheless I shall let that myth go,
For I do not wish to cling to what is false.
I wish to embrace what is genuine.

I turn away from the mural,
That I might one day gaze upon your true form.

I stop reciting the mantras of contradictory doctrine,
That I might feel your voice flow through me
    And we may be able to have a conversation.

You are not a body to be embraced,
You are a deep force to be delved into.
Meeting you is not done with a shaking of hands
    But an entwining of spirits.
Hearing you is not done through opening our ears
    But opening our heart.

In attuning ourselves to hear the unspoken;
In adjusting our sight to see the unseen
And in sharpening our senses to detect the imperceptible,
We begin to recognize that you are always here with us.

Remaking the pathways of our mind,
Which demand explanation before we can lend acceptance.
We shall free ourselves to understand your existence
    And the reality you work off of,
       Which is based upon the one truth:
          That love—you—
            Is capable of all things.

You—deep river of purifying, nourishing waters.
You—wind that carries whispers from other worlds.
You—great solace from the emptiness we have made.
    I am in need of you.

You—whose body is woven
With threads of coursing spirit,
I have seen you emerge from the backdrop
When the dawning light hits you,
    Highlighting the features
    Of your invisible face.

Walking through the mists,
I feel the drapes and folds
    Of the robes you wear,
    As you envelope me.

In the warm caress of the clear light
    Shining upon my face
    I feel the heat from your body.

You—greatest yet humblest force—
You dwell contently in the background.
While we proclaim our might you,
      In your modesty,
Continue to hold all life in balance.

You—encircling, penetrating presence—
You are the most intense being, yet never overbearing;
The most powerful, yet never dominating;
The wisest, yet without a trace of arrogance about you.
Show me your ways; for I wish to be as you are.

You—whose presence is so powerful—
You hold gravity over my entire being,
Just as the sun and moon hold sway over the ocean.
When I feel you pull away my soul recedes
And when I feel you come near the tide floods in
                            And depth returns.

Yet you never pull away, do you.
It is always I who leaves…
I who allows myself
To be taken away by that other current
      —Swept from you—
   Pulled back into the shallows,
To be beached upon the barren world
        We, mankind, have created.

What we create, reflects what lies within us.
You—venerable, learned teacher—you knew this.

You went forward slowly,
    Growing until you were ready
And then you brought forth the earth from your soul—
    A creation which shows the beauty of your inner-self.
While we, in our haste and greed,
    Built a world upon your earth
That reflects our ugliness and arrogance.

Show us our beauty, great mirror.
Let us look through your ancient lens
    And see the earth as you do,
That we might pause in solemn respect
And not thoughtlessly destroy the perfection
        You so painstakingly brought forth.

While others seek dominion over the earth, know this:
I do not wish to create my own world.
I wish only to be free to explore every depth of yours.

I would be forever content
To dwell in the vastness of your soul.
Wandering through the many rooms
    Within your grand house.
To put away the endeavors of concrete and steel,
And lay my head in the beds of thick grass,
At the bases of the elder trees,
Beneath the vaulted loft of the flowering branches.

Gazing upon each bloom,
    Beholding each vista,
        Watching each living creature,
All the while knowing that as I do
I am looking upon the different sides of you.

You whose soul is the prism that,
    When the light of the sun passes through,
Creates the rainbow,
I wish to pass myself through you,
    That I may see the multicolored hues
        That compose the fiber of my being.

I wish to leave behind
This black and white world of sharp angles
    That we created in our narrowness
And step into the vibrant world of flowing contours,
        Which you created in your boundlessness.

Are you there oh silent one,
Listening to my pleas?
Are you here with me
As I mutter in the darkness?

How I wish for you to take form beside me.
While, all along, you sit beside me wishing for me
To be able to see that you already have.

Will this ever end?
Will this wall that lies between us
    Ever come down?
I do not know what creates it.
I do not think it is my disbelief;
For I am here reaching for you—
        Who I know is there.

Tell me knowledgeable one:
What makes the unseen, unseeable?
Is it something in its nature
Or something in ours?

Why would the creation
Not be able to see the creator?

We have tried to relate to you
By giving you our own image.
We gave you the image of the bearded man,
That we might have a face for the presence
We have sensed just beyond
    And so ardently sought to know.
But, perhaps you are not to be found in body.

You gave us the vessel
    In which to hold our being woven of spirit.
But perhaps, you desired no such house for your own being.
Choosing instead to keep yourself in free flowing spirit,
Ever-migrating through the channels of the unseen,
That you might be with all of us at once.

If we are to find you
We must look for what a being is
    When out of its body.
If we are to depict you,
We must draw what we are
When removed from this vessel.

To find the part of you that is within us,
We must first look upon our true form.
To find the family resemblance
We must look in the mirror that reflects the internal—
Look beyond the features of the body,
    To the face of the being within.

It is there—beyond the surface—
That we shall see the form you take
And know who and what we have always been.

It is then that we shall realize,
That to find something or *someone*
There is a superficial layer
That must first be peeled back.

It is then that we shall appreciate
    The life that dwells beneath and within.

And when at last we do this,
    The world you created shall open to us
        —The wall will fall away—
And we each shall wake to find you sitting beside us;
Dwelling in that part of the world
We left long ago to pursue other ambitions,
Where you have remained in constant vigil waiting for us
        —Your lost family—to return.

Coming Home

I shall come to you—
    The one who has been waiting
    Faithfully for our return.

Fleeing this morbid city
My exodus shall bring me back
Unto that woodland glen
I roamed before entering this life.

That womb of indistinct, gathering forms and opaque light
    Where you first happened upon me
    And spoke of a thing called *fellowship*
    And a place called *home*.

There among the shadowed trees
Where I first saw you emerge from behind the veil
I shall meet you once more
    And go back with you into your world.

Without regret
I shall leave behind the life
I have tried to make upon this barren plain,
    Returning to that provincial life I once had with you.

No longer shall I lie in this restless sleep.
No longer shall I pretend that this half-life is a full.

Pulling a dark velvet cloak around me,
    Leaving everything behind without a word,
I come to you…I return to you
    —The one who is dearest to my heart.

Through the dank streets of this post-industrial
    —Post-apocalyptic world—
    Past society's armed sentries,
    And through that hidden arched gate that all of us
    Who have chosen to return to you have used,
        I come.

I travel with all haste along the overgrown paths,
Hoping that nothing has befallen you in my absence.
…Hoping that you have not given up on me;
Begging within my panicked heart as I rush towards you,

That you will not deny me this homecoming.
I know you—you whose heart
    Has not the ability to hate.
I know you will not hide from me.
I know you will not deny me this reunion.

I can feel where you are at this very moment.
    …I know where I shall find you.
You are in that place where you toil and pace
    During those long hours
When none of us will listen to you.

Do you sense me as I hurry towards you?
When the final choice was made in my heart
Did a longtime weight lift from your own?

You who have sat awake in worry
Ever since that day we all departed—
Is my homecoming able to relieve some small fraction
    Of the wound we inflicted that day
        When we left you behind?

I hope.

Every day I caused you heartache
Is a day I want to be able to care for you.

Every day you have sat in vigil waiting for us
Is one I want to give back to you filled with joy.

You—the steady heart.
You—the unwavering care.
You—the first, and now the last
    Innocent being upon this earth—
    What you have done for us
    ...What we have done to you.

What can I do to ease you—you
Who have endured the excruciating agony
                     Yet made no sound?

You—in your infallibility—
Are one who no one ever thinks to care for.
There is nothing that can defeat you—this I know.
But that does not mean nothing causes you pain
Or that a loving presence does not bring you comfort.

You are all-powerful
But you are not beyond feeling.
No being is beyond loneliness.
No being is beyond the desire to be loved.

Out of a love for you I have made my choice.
I come home to you this night—
    Not that you might care for me
But that I might care for you.

You—the only being not born from the womb—
You came into existence alone,
    In that beginning before the beginning.

You are the father who had no father of his own.
The child who had no mother.

Are you truly the inexhaustible one?
Do you never diminish,
    No matter the immensity of the burden you bear
    Or the duration in which you endure its strain?
Are you truly the ever-flowing source of strength,
        Which needs nothing to replenish it?

I do not know.
You are a loving being,
    As such you are a source of love.
Yet by the same hand,
This means you are also one
Who needs to be given love to survive.

Just as the human body
Needs food for nourishment and air to breathe,
    So too a loving being
        Needs the care of another to sustain it.

When we turn to you—oh parent of us all—
    To whom do you turn?
When we beseech you for wisdom,
To whom do you look to for council?
Could you truly be one who needs no other?
And if so, how then can you be a being of love?

When we left you alone,
We may as well have left you to die.
In pulling away from you,
We left your heart to starve.

But of course, being the one you are,
    You did not die.

Kept and at the same time cursed by your immortality
    You suffered, yet lived on;
Bearing the weight of your grief alone
After enduring the death of the dreams you had for us—
    The family humanity was meant to be.

Obsessed with the idea of the world we wanted to build
And altered by the sinister need to dominate,
    We were made numb to everything else—even you.

You are our parent
Yet you are also the foundling we cast off.

We dismissed the world you gave us as worthless,
Dismantled it—stripped it of its natural resources
And divided up the vastness into fenced-off plots—
    Leaving you behind to suffer in your isolation
    And dwell on the bitter ironies.

Yet, despite the hurt and frustration you must have felt,
You did not abandon the home we once shared.
Instead you stayed there,
Determined to keep alive all that we had discarded,
So that we might have something to come back to
    On that inevitable day
    When we realized the emptiness of our pursuits.

What makes you the person that you are?
    —Willing to do so much
    …Able to go so far?
Is it your being that is perfect
Or is it your love for us?

Your strength is inexhaustible
Because your devotion is unending.
It is not your composition that is flawless,
                It is your love.

Yet despite your ability to bear all things alone,
I shall not let you do so any longer.

That inevitable day of realization has come,
Clear-headed and heart aflame with a rekindled love,
      I come home.

Grief-stricken by my acts,
Unraveled by the regrets that tug at me,
I return to pick up what I cast off.

I shall take up a place at your side,
    Dear adored Father.
Ignoring my own fatigue
I shall come to your aid.

I shall return to you
To join you as you sit in vigil
Through this darkest night, which we conjured,
    In a hope that I might be able to relieve
    Some portion of your burden.

I shall pull you away from that window
    Overlooking the bleak horizon
Where you have stood
    Ever-waiting,
    Ever-watching,
    Ever-worrying
…Ever-wanting some figure to appear in the distance,
Signaling that one of us might at last be coming home.

I shall take up that guttering candle
    You lit on that fateful day,
Sling one of your wasted arms around my shoulder
And take as much of your heartache upon me as I can bear.

I shall lead you down that long hall unto your room;
Draw back the blankets upon the bed
    And lay you down to rest.

I shall sit with you, oh bereaved Father,
Stroking your creased brow
Until your strained eyes close
And you are eased into the solace of sleep.

Then, I shall light a torch
    From that unwavering flame,
Lock the house tight,
    So that no demons may reach you
And go back out into the night,
Making a pilgrimage to the only other who is as you are,
    So to learn what may be done to help you.

I shall go to the one who knows you best.

To learn what will ease the deep wounds
    You have suffered at our hands,
I shall go to the one
Who has been with you since the beginning.
    —The other sage, the other creator—
And I shall ask her for guidance in trying to heal you
    —The one who none of us can bear to lose.

I shall go speak with my biological mother—the earth.
She is the only other omnipresent.
She is your other half.
The one who, in her vastness,
    Can support you in yours.

In your unseen form
You travel through her unseen planes.
You have passed through her every layer
    —From core to crust and all that lies in-between.
You know intimately each leaf to bloom upon her,
    Every plant to take root into her
    And every being to dwell atop her.

If you—oh solitary greatness—
Were to have a union it would be with her.

Perhaps she truly is your wife
And we simply were not there
To bear witness to the joining.

Perhaps in those ages before life began
There was a binding of you and her,
After which, you both set out together
To bring forth life—she the mother, you the father.
…She the womb where all would grow,
You the heart who could impart the first seeds.

Many have mistaken her for dead,
    Just as many have dismissed you as imaginary,
Contending that if a brain cannot be located
Then there is no consciousness—no intelligence.

Never understanding that,
With certain living beings,
There is no fixed center of awareness;
For some creatures have a heart and a mind
That can be in many places at once—
Moving through the unseen as a nomadic transient spirit
    In which the source of life is contained.

This is the case with you, oh arcane soul.
Yet this is also the existence had by the earth.

You both know what it is
To be alone in your greatness.
You both know what it is
To be misunderstood by that which you bore.

Along with you, aged Father,
She is the most ancient life and has gathered
Much wisdom throughout her days.
So I shall go to her this night.
Traveling unto one of the places
Where I can feel her the strongest,
That I might hear her clearly in her reply.

Making my way unto a thin place
    —Shrouded mountain top
    Ivy-draped ruins or turbulent shore's edge—
I shall appeal for an insight to be given to me
From within her untold stores of gathered wisdom.

I shall tell her I am caring for our beloved—hers and mine.
And see if she cannot impart to me an ancient incantation
Or the ingredients for a soothing balm
    That can be applied to your raw soul.

Elemental Mother, I call to you;
For we the children have hurt him…hurt you both
And I have come home wanting to undo the damage.

I beseech you, oh reclusive medicine woman…
What might I do to close the wound?
Tell me what I might say to fill the hole left in him
    By all those days when we did not speak.
What might I do to heal our family?
What might I do to heal you, who we ravaged
And he, who we disowned;
For I realize now the wrongs done
And have returned to atone for them.

We were so blind,
    So ungrateful,
    So misguided,
    So selfish…so savage.

To doubt the power of love to fulfill us
    —To leave the simple ways
    And to choose instead
    To take up the ambition to conquer—
Was the ultimate insult to you.

Yet even as hurt as you were
In the wake of our choice,
    You did not spite us.

As we the children,
Rose up to tell you our father
That you were wrong in the life you lead,
You did not slap us down.
Such an act never even occurred to you.

Bewildered, brokenhearted, betrayed and abandoned
You watched as we went in our own direction.

You knew then where that path would lead.
You knew where we would bring ourselves.

How did you not go mad
As you watched us build
What would lead to our own end?

Did you scream and rave till your voice gave out,
In a vain effort to give the warnings
We would never allow ourselves to hear?

What you must have gone through
As you watched us desecrate your sacred earth.
Grasping and clutching at yourself
    —Distraught and enraged—
As we raped the purity
You brought forth and held highest.

I do not know how you could forgive us
For destroying all that is sacred to you;
Nevertheless, I know you do.

I come to you now, Father and Mother,
To help mend the family tree
We uprooted in our maelstrom of defiance.

I come to help you clean up
The aftermath that our ignorance
Has left in its wake.

My selfish ambitions
    Blinded me
    But I am clear once more.

Returning to my senses
After the numbness my obsession caused
I look behind me to see the natural laws that we have violated.
Shame, horror and remorse sicken me.
I realize the sacredness of what we harmed
And I cannot live if it is to die as a result of my acts.

Show me what to do
To mend the bond between us.

Let us start over again.
    Show me the world
        As it is through your eyes
So that I might finally be able to see all that I never could.

I once again begin to appreciate
The true worth of all the things around me,
    Which I had shamefully forgotten
        During that bout of madness
            All we children suffered.

Inherent Knowledge

We left behind our belief in the family
    And rejected the notion
        That a simple life could be fulfilling.
We abandoned our stewardship of the natural
So to be free to build the inanimate.

Then, later,
When we could not shed
The nagging sense of emptiness,
We attempted to create new beliefs
To take the place of the old faith we sacrificed
                To our modern pursuits.

But to no avail;
The holes within us continued to fray.

The difference between our world
    And the old world—your world—
Is the difference between the synthetic and the natural.

These substitutions we created
Seem so foreign to me now
    …So transparently false.
These doctrines never quelled our depression.

The deeper I went into these man-made faiths
The more starved for meaning I became.
        These faiths that are permeated
          By a grasping, maddening desperation
              To touch a divine being,
        Who is seemingly always out of reach.
        Driving its followers to emotional extremes
        Or else unto an early death by disbelief.

Perhaps the answer lies in the simple truth
That the distant reverence of the abstract concept
Cannot compare to the fulfillment had
From daily contact with a loving presence.

I was raised with the modern myth
    The old-world truths all but lost.
As such the myth seemed real.

Trumpets, pearl gates, and archangels;
      Forked-tongued demons,
        Brimstone and the great seducer…
Strangely it once seemed so real, so reasonable
—The unquestioned reality of the divine realm.

Yet now that I have seen you…
Now that I have glimpsed the divine in the green
And begun to recall the organic ordinary nature of the sacred
I have slowly come to see those other beliefs as a mythos.

The parables we penned are put to shame,
When compared to the staggering majesty of the natural world.
    Religion versus spirituality....
    Worship versus relationship....
    The synthetic versus the natural....
It is the difference between the holy waters,
    Pooled inert within a slick, marble pedestal bowl,
Which does not ever absorb the warmth of what surrounds it;
And the pure clear, newly melted waters
    That flow down from secluded mountain peaks,
    Along riverbeds that were carved out
    Before the era of man,
    By forces far beyond us.

It is the difference between
    Envisioning the white light
    Shed from the theorized divine orb
And bathing in the warm beams
Radiating down from the sun above,
The consistent presence of which denotes
    More than just a mechanical cycle
But a visible show of fidelity to the life it supports.

I begin to see it now,
All that you once tried to show me.
I begin to remember it now,
All that I once knew when I was innocent.

Over time,
We have gotten so lost within our fictions
       That we have forgotten reality.

We have gotten so lost in our synthetic world
     And have become so used to the despair it causes
That we have forgotten the fullness that can be had
From the interaction between two beings.

Yet what we have done
To bring ourselves to this place
       Is of no matter now.
It is not time for apologies;
The sincerest remorse is expressed
In the changes we make to right the wrong.

It is not the time to wallow and blame
        But to rally
And face what we have long denied.

So starved for meaning
That we are driven into obesity.
We are infected by a uselessness and despair
That has metastasized into a terminal bitterness.

For the health of our heart and our home
We must make a change.

We need to concede that
Underneath the temporary wonder
Of each new novelty,
And behind the painted façade
We animate ourselves with each day,
        Rages an emptiness.

Scoffing at our rustic roots,
We build machines to relieve us of our chores
    Of household and husbandry
    That we might be free
    To pursue the civilized endeavors
    Of society and industry.

Only on our deathbeds
Realizing that the home we build
And the family we cherish
Are the only things of any consequence.

The cure for our modern maladies
    Is dirt under the fingernails
        And the feel of thick grass between the toes.
The cure for our listlessness
    Is to be out within the invigorating wind.
The cure for our uselessness
    Is to take back up our stewardship;
For it is not that there has been no work to be done,
We simply have not been attending to it.

We must confess the emptiness we feel
And embrace our disillusionment.
Speak the unspoken
And admit that our faith
In the virtue of the modern ways
        Has been shaken.

The change will undoubtedly be abrupt,
        Even though we have worked up to it.
It will be extremely trying,
        Even though it is vitality needed.
But it will nonetheless happen—
We will leave this industry-driven world we created,
    Along with all the illusions
        With which we tried to fill the hollowness of it
And we will return to the flourishing shores of the homeland
To become the peasants we once were.

Throughout the ages
Stories have become truth;
While what is real has been forgotten.

The difference between religion and myth
Is not a matter of what is truth and what is fiction,
         It is a matter of time.

History is composed through a combination
         Of extrapolation and fabrication.
Caught within the degrading current of time
And passed down by the distortive tongue of man,
         Truth becomes myth
              And myth, truth.

The Greeks once believed in their gods
And the Egyptians in theirs.
What we would call their *mythologies*
         Would, by them,
              Be called their *religions*
—Gods they lived to appease and died to honor
         Just as we have lived and died for ours.

We create fictitious things
To fill real holes.
We weave together myths to capture
Ideas of divine power
Forgetting that we need not create it;
   For the sacred lives outside our imagination.
Never appreciating that the simple truth
Is so much more moving than our enacted dramas
And elaborate legends could ever be.

Mankind seeks pomp
Around that which we would worship
Yet the wonder of the sacred
Lies within its profound simplicity.
The sacred needs not
Embellishments to bring it forward and give it worth.
It only needs one with eyes able to see the extraordinary
Within what they have gazed upon each and every day.

To find the meaning in our own lives....
To discover the nature of the world we dwell in....
To know our origin and our full potential....
To be comforted by the truth that we are not alone....
To justify that our existence is not without purpose
                      —We seek out the sacred.

All of us believers in meaning,
Seek out the being that embodies it.
Some search for decades and,
    Feeling as though there is nothing to find,
They carve an idol to fill the void—
Desperately wanting it to have the power
To push back the rising fear that life is shallow.

Sacredness
    —A manifestation of purity, of deeper meaning,
    Of fulfillment and of untold wisdom—
These things…these people exist,
They are simply overlooked
By those who seek out the burning bush.
    …We cannot see the sacred lying prostrate
    Before the lifeless effigy.
    …We will not meet the divine if we look only
    For the figures bathed in unworldly light,
All the while staring right through
Those bringers of meaning who stand beside us
And the natural sacredness that blooms around us.

In our needy search for you
We have turned to the celestial heavens
    And the grandiose legends.
Forgetting that the sacred
      Is not pompous,
        It is not anointed;
It is natural, it is simple,
    And it is abundant.

The sacred is to be found within and around—
    Coming to appreciate this fully
    Is the great awakening, which brings the insights
    That transcend our mundane lives
    To become a journey through an extraordinary realm.

To discover the divine
    We must see the ordinary with new eyes of appreciation.

The sacred is found in the seemingly mundane.
It is found at home;
We contain a piece of it within the four walls
We build to protect those we hold dear.
And when there is love
Between those who dwell within,
Our small piece of sacredness
Shall be encouraged to grow,
Spreading to every corner
    —Penetrating the very foundation—
Making our home a chapel
Within the greater cathedral of the world.

We can imbue what we create with love
And in doing so make it sacred.
Yet the wild divinity
    —That which was here before us
    And grows without need of our help—
Is rooted in the Earth herself.

There are those things we are taught are sacred
But then there are those things that
We have always sensed to have significance.
…Those moments and those places
That by nature humble us—
    Invoking within us
    That silent, private reverence
When our mind hushes,
Our self-importance recedes
    And our soul yields
    As we behold in awe
What we inwardly know to be divine.

There are those thing
That we were taught to bow before
    But then there are those things which,
When we come before them,
    We instinctually drop to our knees;
For we know that we have come
Into the presence of what is holy.

We find sacredness
While walking through the wood
Where the thick trees tower
    —Having grown for millennia—
Their ancient roots digging deep into the Earth,
Winding their way toward the soul of her.

We brush against the sacred
As we walk amongst the tall barley
—Its heavy tips bowing and rolling in the wind.

We are inundated by it
As we journey through the fog
That floods into the lush green valley at dawn

We experience its intensity
In the locked gaze
    Of the sixteen point stag standing proudly
    —His doe and fawn poised behind him.

We behold it in the powerful
Yet elegant movements of the whale with her calf
As they pass through the brackish white capped waters
    To crest the surface
        —Where they take in a breath—
Then together plunge back down
    Into the unreachable places once more.

The sacred is glimpsed
In the breathless, transient appearance
Of the bejeweled hovering hummingbird.

It is felt in the building stillness
Before the first snow descends each winter.
It lives at the roots of the first tree to open its leaves
           And fulfill the renewal of spring.

It can be experienced in the summer rain that falls
    From a cloudless sky,
        Leaving the vapor of a rainbow in its wake.

The sacred is partaken of
As we bite into the crisp, sweetly ripened flesh
    Of the harvest's first fruit.
Or when we use the season's first wheat to
Make a round loaf of bread,
Pull it brown and crisp from the stone hearth
And tear it by hand to share amongst our family.

Sacredness resounds
In a voice that expresses the sentiments of the heart,
Whether in whispered words said unto a lover
Or sung in verse melodies that ring out to be heard by all.
It reverberates from the plucked harp
    And the strummed guitar.
It carries from the carved flute
    And the pounded calfskin drum.

Sacredness trails behind the brush
    Moving smoothly across the canvas
And drips from the tip of the dipped quill.

The sacred is happened upon
When we find the spiraling conch shell washed up intact
    Upon the grainy shores of sun-warmed waters.

It can be seen
In the pine tree where the snowy owl perches,
    Its golden eyes looking into our soul.

It can be witnessed
In the long graceful steps of the great blue heron
    Stalking along the banks of the still pond.

It can be heard
In the symphony of the crickets
Echoing back and forth to one another
    On a warm summer's eve.

It can be absorbed
From the sound of the running brook
Passing over the smoothed stones,
As its cool waters trickle towards
    The mouth of the wide-brimmed lake.

We left you behind because we thought
our modern endeavors would make us more.
We wove the myths to fill the holes left when we abandoned
Our belief in the old ways of hearth, home and harvest,
Which paid reverence to the holiness of the land
And the preciousness of those we share our sojourn upon it with.
    …The ways that held all things in balance
    And allowed us to move through this world with grace.

In the generations to pass
Since our departure from the village
We have forgotten what true sacredness is.

Yet many of us have gone in search of it—
Trying to rediscover the world lost
And tap the inherent knowledge
    Contained within us as your children.

That yearning to reconnect with you
Has carried over from one generation to the next.
While there have been those who have sought you out
In a desire to strip from you the wealth of your creation
And employ your power to their own ends,
Many of us have sought you out
In need of your company
    And an affirmation of your love and forgiveness.

We wrote the myths
And over time forgot they were our fictions.

No longer remembering your original name
Among the many we have superimposed upon you,
We have called out for you using the names
We gave to the holy characters within our tales.

Desperate to feel a connection to you….
We have taken up the symbols of our modern religions—
    A different geometrical shape to define
    Each different way we tried to reshape you.
Yet there is no power to be found in
The symbols we create
…No power in these synthetic things to which we cling.

We go outside ourselves
For our connection to you.
We loop around our hands the rosaries
And through the chain of plastic spherical beads
Made in our factories,
We channel our pleas to you.

Nonetheless, these talismans we made
Have power within our mind alone;
The strand of beads does not run
 From our hands to your heart.
It is merely an object through which
We would send our love to you.
…An object that we think
We needed in order to be heard.

But no more.

As I walk away from this artificial world we have made,
I leave my own worn beads behind—
    Coiled on the doorstep of the church
    To which I shall never return.
Now to channel all the love I have for you
And all the words I would say to you
Through my heart alone.
      …The part of my own being
      That is inherently connected unto you.

After the Night, Before the Day

I have sought the sacred
And found that it surrounds.
Yet where are you, oh arcane soul, first to draw breath.

There are times when you feel so close
    That, if I only look up
I might see you moving towards me.
Still there are other times
When you are so far away
That you seem to inhabit
My dreams alone.

There are those times, those places,
In which I am able to feel you near.
The most hallowed of all
Being that of sunrise and sunset.

Sacredness is experienced
    Where day meets night,
    And night meets day.

The hours of convergence
    Where the two opposites meet
And blend into each other,
Creating the blurred boundaries
Of half-light and twilight,
Where we can walk through
That space in-between dreams and reality.

I know that it is not I alone
Who appreciates the solemnness of these times.

You imparted to us the inherent knowledge
    Of the holiness of these hours
And they have been the first places
Many of us have gone to in search of you.

Into these times of day we searchers
Make sojourns into the dawn
Leaving behind the drudgery,
Hoping for a respite
    Wherein we might lay our weary heads
    Upon your strong breast and, in the calm,
    Listen for the beat of your heart.

These hours are the moments of in-between;
For it is neither night nor day,
It is neither yesterday nor the day to come.
There is no past, no future,
Only the moment of the breathing present
              And our need for you.

These hushed hours of serene dimness and diffused hues,
When the last day is unbound from its body
And the new day is gathered—
    Woven together before our eyes
        With strands of pure light itself.

These thin places within each day have drawn me so
—Pulling me from bed early and keeping me up late—
Because they have always been the brief intervals
When I am able to meet you;
As if these two times of day are periods of eclipse
Wherein the two worlds upon this one earth align
And I am able to reach through the opening and touch you,
                Even if only for the briefest of moments.

The sun and moon remain constant
Between all realms of this earth—
    Stretch the distance between worlds.

I live knowing
That we work under the warm light of the same sun
And sleep under the same blanket of night
And in this I am consoled.

When I go into the widening-sphere of emerging light
I feel as though I am taking in the sun
As it passes from your hands—you the one I love
    But cannot yet fully be with.
Cherished, I clutch this gift
    —This new day you have given me—
To my chest, vowing to waste not a moment of it.

Having risen at dawn and lingered till dusk,
    I may say I know this day.

I watched the day come forward from out of the mist.
I watched as the darkness yielded
And the clean light steadily intensified.
I was there for the beginning and the end—
    There as the light struck the earth
      And there when it faded from it.

At sunrise I came to know
An already familiar friend anew.
And at sunset I watched her leave.
Remembering I knew her for as long as I could.
From the moment she drew her first breath—
    Shining her first rays into the darkness.
Till the moment she exhaled
And her luminous soul sank beneath the edge of the world;
As she went on to rise in another place to meet you,
    Who has been waiting through the night,
      Longing to see her return.

The other side to the sacred day
Is the transcendent, surreal period of night—
The time when the body sleeps and the spirit awakens.

Each morning I take the new day from your hands,
As if it was a child newly passed from your womb,
Then each evening I give it back to you.

And it is as I let the spent day
Slip through my slackening grip
That I feel our hands meet,
As you give unto me the mystical time of night.

The consecrated hours during which my dreams
Can come out from their sheltered hiding place
To take a breath in the open air
And my homesick spirit may work
To journey across the distance between us.

When the sun has risen on your shore
And you take to your daily work.
I lie down into the cradle of dreams
And envision the life we shall have
When I make it home to the place you are.

During the daylight I survive
But at night I live.

As my hands are relieved of their toilsome daylight duties
I once again resume my search for you.

I find I am able to make the most
Progress towards you in the dim;
For the greatest thoughts come in that cradle of night—
    Contemplated by moonlight,
      And written by the glow of the candle,
As the backward world, sleeps
And I dream of the world that still can be.
…That should be. …That once was.
…The world that I live only to return to.

The Language of the Mute

I would tell you
Just how deep my longing goes,
    If only I could find a pen
        Worthy of transcribing such intimate love.

The voice of the sacred
Is channeled through the written word—
        When we take up the old tools of hand-cut quill,
        Steeped oak gall ink and molded cotton paper,
And let the words of our soul pour out
And be absorbed into the surface of the parchment.

The paper accepting
All that we are able to draw forth
    From the well of emotion
Running deep through the center of our being,
Forgiving sins named
And keeping quiet the confidences shared.

I have attempted to convert my ineffable emotion into words;
Keeping running journals of all the fragments
I have thus far been able to translate.

The shelves that line my walls
Are filled with scrolls I would give to you
               If only I could find you.

Hand-stitched books
Weight the tables within my house—
Volumes filled with letters I wrote to you,
        Questions I have posed to you
And gathered notations of whispers
I have overheard while traveling in your wake.

Whether bearing an inner-confession
Or chronicling the journey we have made,
Taking up the pen and setting it to paper is a sacred act;
For it brings forth the unexpressed to be known
Making our innermost emotion tangible,
As we release our declarations to the page,
    And put them in the hands of another.

Since the birth of the light, night and air
We have toted tablet, papyrus and scroll
And throughout that time the blank page
Has become something different to each of us.
    It has been the priest willing to hear our confession
    And the confidant willing to keep our secrets;
    It has been a kindred spirit willing to take in
    All the dreams we long to share;
    The counselor that always listens intently
    And the teacher who lets us
    Come to our own conclusions.

Approaching the pen
    Is more revealing than approaching the mirror.
    …More cleansing than a baptism.
    …More medicinal than a pill.

Approaching the pen
Is likened to drawing forth the soul
From the protection of the body
       —Causing it to be utterly exposed.

Through the written word
Our mute soul speaks all that it has longed to say.

All feeling yet no voice,
Our soul grasps at the pen wanting to be known,
To be heard…to be released.

Language might have had humble beginnings—
Created merely to help life's most basic daily interaction.
Yet somewhere throughout the ages this changed,
As humanity took up the written word, not for function,
But with passion and need
   —Using it to declare who we are—
Transcending language to become
A tool of the innermost self.

Our mute soul
Extends itself to the pen
And joins to the page
So to have a means of voicing
What it alone has seen, sensed, undergone
                          And yearned for.

The pen lends voice to the parts of us that suffer silently.
Our muted dreams that burn and wane silently within us
Channel their anguish through the mournful black ink.

The pent up love we have for the family yet to be found
Overflows onto the page,
    Where thankfully it is taken,
Saving us from drowning within its obstructed intensity.

Our soul mouths silent words to us
In an effort to communicate its realizations—
    Truth that we can sometimes come to understand
    Through intuition alone.

Yet when we give our soul the instrument of the pen,
Rest under our hand a blank sheet of paper,
    Disconnect the inhibiting brain
And let the heart's confidence be a force of encouragement,
We at last behold the transcribing of all the truths
    Our soul has stored within it.
…We are able to read a transcription
Of the whispers our soul hears
    Resonating from across the distance,
Through the gulf of the unseen we wish to cross.

Our soul desires a vessel that can hold its wisdom;
The blank book and full pen can be such a vessel.

Yes, for some parts—some entries made—
It feels as though the extent of our language
Does not reach far enough
To convey the intended depth.
Nonetheless, we need not abandon
The recording of these ineffable depths
We must learn a new language…rather, we must
Recall the olden one.

The one whose tongue died out long ago;
Spoken now only by a few devotees.
    …The language that holds within it
        The words for divine description.

The language of our native land,
Whose meaning is not simply conveyed
In the shape of the letters
But in the passion with which we write them
And the conviction with which we stand by them.

The language whose etymology
Stems from the silent dialect we use
When we are spun-spirit alone—
No body, no vocal cords
    Yet possessing a voice nonetheless.

A language whose words
Can be written only by those
Who transcribe the voice
    Resonating within the fibers of their being.
Adding within each word an underlying layer of meaning,
As heart and hand act as one and all heed our soul
That has at last come forward to tell us who we are.

Original Form

For untold lifetimes we have been searching for you
       And for our purer selves.

We wander through this world
On an interminable search for truth,
Unsure as to what it actually looks like;
With a mysterious amnesia that has left us
Without memory of who we are,
       Where we originated
And all that we once learned at your knee.

As we became less human
Was the inherent knowledge
You imparted to us
As one of your descendants, lost?

As we became the synthetic,
    —As we became the machine,
   As we became the lie—
Did we diverge into another creature?
Was the wisdom of our original self lost?

Was our memory lost over our gradual descent
From children of the divine
    To the hoggish creatures we are now?

Does the inherent knowledge
Lie in our bones or in our humanity?
    …In our blood or in our purity?

When we chose to leave our indigenous roots behind,
It was more than a declaration, wasn't it.

It was an act of physically changing ourselves—
    Erasing who we once were
So to be free to establish
Who we would make ourselves to be.

Perhaps it was this act that caused the amnesia.
    …Perhaps it was done by our own hand.
    …I am not sure.

I do not know what caused the loss of identity—
Whether it was our own doing
    Or something that was done.
But I do know that not all of us want to remain this way.
Many of us earnestly seek to return to our original selves.
And it is you—the one who can recall
      What we were like when we were children—
            Who can help us do so.

We explore the sacred realm
    Upon these two feet,
    With these two hands.

We feel our way blindly over the surface of the Earth—
    Passing our hands over her face
    Trying to recognize her beauty.
…Trying to recall our biological mother.
…Trying to recognize the sparse truths
   Among the vast illusion.

We try to find some trace of you—
   Tracking you through the dense wood
Like a mythical creature we need to know is real;
Looking for a leaf you might have bent in passing
Or a trail of prints left upon the forest floor,
Which would lead us to the place
    Where you lay your head each night.

Yet why not unfurl this body
And let us delve into the earth's many layers
          As you do?

We are, as you are—oh boundless being.
You bore us and when you did
You imparted all that you are unto us.
You did not make a lesser being to govern,
But an equal to embrace.

You did not fear what we would become.
You did not hoard power as we might have.
You—the loving being that you are—
Live to see those around you flourish.
And so you gave us all that you could
In a hope that we might have
A chance to become even more.

So then, with this inheritance ensured,
What prevents us from living as you do
    —Infinite, flowing, omnipresent?

What traps us? Is it this skin?
No.
Our disbelief is what imprisons us.
The vastness of your being
    Is due to the immensity of your belief.
While our smallness
    Is the result of our inability to.

Help me, oh pious one.
Bolster my anemic faith
With a transfusion of your confidence.
Make the complex, simple.
Make the impossible, easy.

Help me see that the improbable
Can still come to pass.
Release me from the isolating confines
Of my limited ability to trust.
Unbind me from this suffocating doubt.

Let me revert to my original form.
Let my unraveling being mingle with yours.
Let me shed this body and race you on the wind
To the place on this earth where the sun is now rising.
Let me feel what it is like
To circle within the hurricane of love's force.
Let me feel what it is like to stretch across the breadth of time.
Let me feel what it is to loop around the brim of the galaxy.
Let me feel what it is like to have the fluid fingers of my soul
       Converge with another.

The Two Sides

You—swirling, flowing form
Moving around and through me,
If you will not step into a body at least
Solidify the fog and mist,
And take some shape however vague,
That I might have an incarnation
Of the one I love so deeply,
    Even if only for a moment.

You—deep cradle—
I wish to crawl into your arms.
Tell me everything will be alright.
Tell me I am safe.
Tell me you are here.
And in return I will make that
Most sacred act a heart can—
        I will trust in you.
        …I will believe you.

At day's end
I like to think I come home to you
    —That even in your absence
    Some part of you is with me—
But there are times,
After the day has been difficult,
When I wonder if I'm not
Truly alone in this house.

Is our fate what the pessimists
        Would tell us it is?
Are we alone?
Are you our most loyal companion
Or our most-needed illusion?

Are you there
Or do we simply need you to be?
Have the stories of you
Come forth from profound experience
        Or profound loneliness?

Were you here before us
Or did you come into existence with us—
      We the human being
    And you the meaning we must have
    To give sense to our existence?

I do not wish to converse
With a manifestation of my own despair.
I do not wish to take up a belief in you
          In an effort to fill a hole.
I want to reach out to you,
Not in need but in love.

Was religion founded through our faith
          Or upon the loss thereof?
Sometimes it seems
As though the drama of the Mass
Is not a celebration of our belief
But an overcompensation
To hide a faith that is missing.
As though we feel the need to
Dress you up—adorn you—
In an effort to convince ourselves
That the effigy we carved of you
     Is the image of someone real.

I know not if the tomes were written
By the pious or by the needy.
    ...By the enlightened
        Or by the wishful.

I know not if the apparitions of you
Have been your efforts to reach us through the unseen.
Or simply a worsening of our own desperation,
    During which we suffered
    Momentary hallucinations.

Is our belief in you
Our saving grace or fatal flaw?
...Our strength or our frailty?

I know what the broken man would say;
    For I know what I have said
    When at my lowest point,
        In those unforgivable moments
        When I condemned you for your apathy
        Or dismissed you as a delusion of a naive child.

However, I also know
What my heart has told me from the very beginning.
I know the truth I always come back to—
    The love that never leaves me.
I only wish I understood our situation better.

When I was younger
I never questioned the realness of you.
How confident that child was.
…How frail they have been left.

   Adrift
—Becalmed within this long stretch of doubt—
I try to reach the shores of home, though
Have not the momentum of belief to carry me there.

We enter this world certain
               And yet,
The longer we are here
The less certain we become.

Shouldn't it be the other way around?
Perhaps.
    But then again,
Perhaps not.

Maybe we enter this world
Certain in the existence of the unseen
Because some unconscious part of us
Remembers dwelling briefly
In that layer of the world before birth.
Yet once we passed from that place
The memory faded from us with time,
              Just as all memories do.

Did I know you once?
Did we ever stay up
Late into the night in conversation?

Is that why I sit up now—
 Does some part of me
Mourn that time we once spent together?

Was there a time when I knew your name?
Was there a time when I understood your workings?
 …Your existence?
Was there a time when I could recall
What it felt like to be held by you?

Was there a time when I actually came home to you
 …When I sat hearth-side with you,
Listening to the stories of all you have witnessed.

If these memories exist somewhere within me
Cannot I reawaken them? ...cannot you?
Isn't there some force that you
Can send surging through me
To reawaken those dormant parts—
To reconstruct those now decayed fragments.
Cannot you make those faded days
     Sharp within my mind again?
Cannot you help me to recall all that I am
        ...All that I have ever been?

Is there not some pulse of renewal
    —Some current of energy—
That can stimulate that dead part of me
And restore that past life to me?

Can you—oh shaman—
Recover those fragments of my soul lost to me?
That I might remember all that we have shared
And know that you are more than
The embodiment of my dreams;
    You are my friend,
      My father, my mother, my lover—
        My past and my future.

Does my longing drive me to create you
Or does it drive me to return to you?
Does the despair come from
The void of what has never been
Or from the anguish of what was once had
But now must be done without?

I do not believe you are a dream;
For I do not believe I could love
      Someone who was merely imagined,
      As deeply as I do you.

I can feel the love I have for you
      Extend from my heart,
Travel to you across the distance
And penetrate every layer of your being
—Bone and blood,
      Marrow and muscle,
           Skin and nerve,
Right to the core of your generous soul.
That is how deep my love goes.
   …That is how real you are.

My love for you
    —My love…not my need—
Is a tangible force gathered at the center of me
    —Settled beneath my sternum,
    Resplendent in its fullness—
And so you too must be just as tangible.

We can need a dream;
The thought of it can give us peace and consolation,
We can depend on it and be defined by it,
We can find joy in the thought of it becoming reality.
But can we love a dream?
A true love—unwavering and unconditional.

I do not love the thought of you.
I do not love an illusion.
I love a person…a being—you.

I cannot recall your name,
I cannot remember precisely
The place where we first met
But I miss you all the same.

I miss, not a vague impression of a deity,
Or a comforting fiction but you—
    The feel of your presence,
        Your humor and insight,
        Your kindness, your care…
           And your embrace.

I have little memory of you
Yet, at the same time, I know you.
Your personality is not an idea
Woven together by my mind
Of who I would hope you to be.

Rather, it is an impression
That has remained within my heart—
    Enduring on in a place
    That teeters on the border
    Between the conscious and unconscious
    And contains knowledge
    That cannot be conveyed nor explained.

Perhaps if these hibernating, wilted memories
Of our time together were verdant once more
These impressions I have of you
—The nameless, the faceless—
Would not drift in the surreal gray area
        Of what might be imagined.

Nevertheless, I can appreciate you
Even without my memories
And love you for all that you
Have done for me in this life,
    Without knowing just
        How far back our history goes.

I love you—that is how I know you are real.

If you were merely a dream…a fantasy,
My love for you would die with my belief in you,
        But it doesn't.
The love between us
Is the one thing that remains
Even after all belief has failed.

My belief in you does not hold up your existence;
You exist independent of my mind…of my need.

We may have maimed your identity
      But we did not create you.
I may reach for you during the desperate times
But that does not mean my desperation bore you.

In the end, it means
Some part of me remembers
That you have never failed me
And knows that you are the one
      Who can save me now.

You are the only one
Who knows what to say to me to calm me.
You are the only one who can inspire me
   —Rouse me from the despondency
   Symptomatic of this age.
You are the only one
Who fully understands the workings of me.

…I reach to you because
You are the one I have always reached to
   …The one who has always come,
     Who I need not explain things to.
   …The one who knows me better than I know myself.

My Return to the New England Wood

I have come back to the paths I roamed as a child
Hoping to find here
The innocent who believed in you so fully.

You—the ever-present yet seldom noticed.
You—the one who is always reaching, yet rarely felt.
You—the one who all us world-weary hearts mourn the loss of.

I search for you,
Though I know now that, if I am to find you,
              I must first find myself.

There was once a child
    Who believed in you wholly
    And without doubt.

How wise this child was
And how undervalued.

How desperately I search for that child now.
Just to hear them speak of you
In that impassioned voice
That only the confident possess.

I return now to the wood
Where that child once roamed
With a hope that walking the old paths
Might revive its dead spirit.
Or the mulchy ground and musty air might act
As a tonic for my jaded soul
That has been overexposed to this poisonous age.

I walk through the stillness
Searching for a divide
In the invisible cloth draped between us,
That I might draw back the curtain
And enter the world in which you dwell.

Deeper into the ancient wood I go
Straining to pick up the whispers of the ancestors
                Riding on the westerly winds.
Pleading to all spirits who know the path unto you,
                                  To guide my feet.

I walk through the woods
Trying to find the trail that will take me into the past.

Along the boundary between the two worlds, I walk;
Retracing the paths I blazed long ago
Searching for the child I abandoned along the way
        Who possesses my true identity.

The woods—the ancient thicket.
Roots bulge through the topsoil,
    Intersecting the path,
    Like thick leathery veins
Running through the body of the earth.

Walking through
The groves of knee-high ferns,
And along the stone walls,
The farm they fenced in is gone.

In the old wheat fields
Now grow the young oak, maple and elm.
The stone foundation of the house
Is all that is left of the homestead.

Longing for a jolt of memory,
I walk back into the old life.
Coming to the house,
I go down the narrow stone steps
That still remain set into the ground,
Descending into what has now become
A cellar of the earth;
    For there is neither roof above me
    Nor frame around me,
Only the dome of summer leaves,
The vaulted beams that are the branches
And the stained-glass skylight above, that is the sun
    Filtering through the few leaves
    That have already turned golden.

Walking on,
I see some of the younger trees have been broken by
The torrent storm that swept through here years before
      And ended up lasting longer
      Than anyone thought it might.

Broken-off at the root,
They have since dried out
Over the harsh winters to follow.
Left propped against the giants around them,
The collapsed saplings rest their heads upon their parent—
    The elder whose seed brought them forth
    And whose roots went deep enough
    To survive the great upheaval.

Such am I—a once promising strong youth,
Now uprooted after the storm
That raged violently for decades;
Leaning against you—the one who manages to weather all.

I have left behind the darkness of my room—
    The confining plaster and cold sheet rock,
    Overbearing roof and barred door,
For the bright openness of the natural world.

I walk the paths
I walked in my youth,
    Though, not for nostalgia.

I came here knowing what I must do.
The guide within said unto me:
    "Find the child. Think them not a fool.
    Follow them. Heed them.
    Return to yourself by embracing
    What you were when innocent.
    Banish the pessimist that has emerged
    In the intervening years
        —Silence him—
    Do not engage him
    Nor justify your belief to him—just know
        And with that knowing, walk away.
            Invoke the idealist!"

And so I came to this wood
Where the idealist once made pilgrimage
            All those years ago.
    Hoping to recover all that I lost.
    …To reclaim all that I left behind.

Follow the beam of light back to its source
And find there the sun
Around which your world revolves.

One thought at a time
We move away from ourselves
And one thought at a time
We return to ourselves.

Somewhere in the deepest chamber of my heart,
Where there is protection and solitude,
    The idealist—the believer—
Lies upon its deathbed trying to recover.
Bound and stitched, sipping clear broth
With the visionaries of generations past gathered in prayer....

The last rites given,
The requiem recited,
None expect this mauled soul to survive.

In a fever of disillusionment the idealist—the child—
Loses themselves and I lose my only hope.
Over time, with my fits of pessimism,
I have weakened its heart.
But now—this day—
As I walk through these woods
Where the child was once so happy
I beg for its strength to be returned.

I come here my child,
Not to mourn the imminent loss of you.
I bring you here to lay you upon the altar stone
And invoke the spirits in the surround
To save you—one who has been their greatest advocate.

I bring you here
As a way to amend the falling out between us,
    Before you are lost to me for good.

I thought you naive for believing as you did
    For trusting so absolutely,
    For expressing your feelings so freely,
    For opening yourself so fully.

I damned you for your naivety,
For your foolish expectations, for your idealism…
For sharing so much
    And for believing it would all be so easy.

And while you were misguided to think bringing change
    To all that is wrong in this world would be easy,
You were not a fool for believing as you did.
You had a strength that I now lack.
    You had a faith that I now need.

When you were left behind,
So too was my goodness and my convictions.
I thought I was ridding myself of a weakness
But truly I was giving up my hope
That life could be better.

I want that belief back now;
    So rise up upon that deathbed
And tell me what it is you remember
Believing all those years ago
    When you were strong
    And possibility was infinite.
Tell me again of the goodness you saw in people
        And the hope you saw for the world.

Save me dear child,
Before I become one of the walking dead
    —Poisoned and embittered.
You are the one who has the power to bring me back.
You are the only one who can spare me the barren fate
        Shared by those who believe in nothing.

Rise up,
Take me by the hand
And lead me through the sacred world
You discovered all those years ago
I am ready to trust
In what you have always known to be real.

Reentering the Womb

Breathing heavily,
Holding the rhythm steadily.
Strained eyes staring unblinking
          —Startling clear.
A gaze held with taut focus,
As the single-minded purpose takes hold.

In this séance I reach out
    Not to a former friend or lost master;
Instead I seek to retrieve my own self—
    To connect with the dead part of myself
    And find how I might revive them.

Casting another log upon the climbing flames,
Sending sparks coiling up into the shadowed canopy,
I push back another inch of intimidating darkness—
Widening the incandescent sphere of protection.

Kneeling down upon the gritty, mulchy forest floor,
With a fallen birch rod I perform the *caim*
    —Drawing a wide circle around me—
  At the center of which I shall lay safeguarded
    And removed from this land
  Where the starved demons hunt me.

All that haunts me
Cannot enter within this circle.
Regret, desperation, loneliness,
    Anger, envy, doubt, fear—
All that torments me
Cannot follow me across this line;
    I may pass within
But all of it must stay on the out.
Within this sanctum I am free to be
The person that I would be
Without the influences and afflictions
        That have altered me.

The figments of my demons
Dance outside this ring
Chanting that which I most fear to hear
But within this sphere I am beyond their reach,
Bringing me all the nearer to you—
    The one whose voice I strain to hear
Above the incessant debating of the doubts within me.

Come sit with me
Within this circle, oh gentle one,
I will let you and only you
Pass through the protective boundary.
Come here and heal the child dying within me,
    I know you have the skills to save it.

I need nothing that lay beyond this ring—
    Not food nor water nor warmth.
I need only protection and a moments peace.
I need only the calm contained within this sphere
And the company of you.

Here I shall fast,
Here I shall pray,
Here I shall heal
    Or here I will die.

Here within this cocoon
    The wounds from the old life shall fade
As new, tougher skin grows
And I emerge with wings strong enough to carry me
Beyond the desolation of my surround.

Fill this circle with your breath
And turn this refuge into a womb.

Let me drift suspended
In the viscous fluid of your clean soul.
Encourage the amputated innocence to re-grow.
Refortify my stretched joints and chipped bones,
Atrophied hope and arthritic dreams.

Let me keep what wisdom I have earned
But let the rest be wiped clean in an evolution of self.
Let me move on to the next life,
    The next form,
    The next place.

You—the elder of us all—
Did you evolve from a being of flesh
Into the incorporeal omnipresent?
Are we what you once were?
Are you what we shall become?

Shall the next evolution of mankind be to shed this skin?
As the soul develops and expands
Does the skin simply peel off this body of spirit?

Sitting here in my claustrophobic life of few choices,
To think that I shall one day have perfect freedom
Makes me drag myself forward unto the next day.

Oh how I shall savor the removal of this suffocating flesh!
I shall simply slip out of this suit
That clothes my naked, homespun soul,
Stretch the stiff bands of energy
That were matted down under the heavy
Elastic layers of muscle and flesh
And delve into the wind—flowing like a river across the hills,
    In-between the trees, through the glens,
        Off the bluff cliffs and across the firth—out to sea.

Here in this womb transform me—transcend me;
Leave the core intact but reshape the body around it.

Let me leave this house and venture out into the open world.
Let me leap from the nest and take flight.

Let me become the potential that is pent-up within me.

Hiraeth

We each seek a rite of passage—
    To be bidden to pass through fire
    Or be plunged into sanctified water.
…To be sent on the vision quest of fasting
Or kept in the darkened sweat lodge where,
    Transported by the chanting of our fellows,
We shall decipher the revelations
Glimpsed within the induced fever.

We all seek to have the metal of our soul tested.
We all wish for that chance
To be initiated into the circle of the sacred.

We all live in need of that defining moment
That will make the lasting distinction
Between the time in our life when we felt alone
And the time when we realized
We are connected to the greater force.

We all long for that pivotal event
That will mark the true beginning of our life…
    When the greater context behind our existence
Will reveal itself and the path beneath our wandering
                    Will become clear.

We each survive—merely survive—
    Waiting for that day
When the life equal to our potential will begin.

We each try to carry on while within this shallow world,
All along yearning to be led into a hidden world of magic
By a guide who arrives knowing the answers to all our questions
And bearing all that we need to fill our wanting soul.

We are born aching for the sacred—
Homesick for the world from whence we came
…Still haunted by the images of the paradise lost.

You—oh keeper of the doorway—
Reach out a hand to us.

You do not hide the sacred world from us.
No, you drape it around us
    Setting it above and below,
      Around and within,
Yet still we cannot see it.

Illuminate the sacred world
You luminescent spirit.
Bring the sacred to our attention.
Make us look up from the unimportant work,
      Which consumes us so.

Wake us from our despondency.
Bring us out of our catatonic hopelessness.
Take hold of us—grab tight—
And shake us till we come to our senses.
…Till we look up at the beauty you created
                With bright eyes of awe.

Send out a cry, you shy force that goes unnoticed;
Go swiftly to your highest mount
And let a call of awakening ring out,
The force of which will strip off the dullness that has built-up
                Upon the brilliant colors of this world.

Be the epicenter of change you—oh mighty heart.
Take hold of yourself, timid one
    And unleash that voice you so seldom use,
That has the potential to stretch as far as you do;
For only you can reach us
    In the depths of the abyss
    Into which we have descended.

I cannot recall all that we were
Nor all that once was.
Yet my yearning for you
    Shows that some part of my heart
    Can still remember what my mind cannot.

On the out, I have been timeworn and world-wearied—
    Left staring impassively
    Out into a world I no longer expect to change.

Yet on the in, my spirit wails in agony—
    Singing the dirge
    As I mourn the life of meaning I sought
    And do not wish to relinquish the hope of knowing.

Do not comfort me.
Do not give me consolation.
Instead, bring to me all
That lay just beyond my reach.

I know you can.

Cannot you feel me
Grasping and pulling on you in my death throes?
    …My starving soul begging you
    For the means to be self-sustaining?

We destroyed all that would have sustained us
    —Uprooting the orchards and damming the springs
    To make way for our barren metropolis—
And now we endure the famine.

Bring me to the center of the Earth
    —That soul of her,
      Which I know you kept safe—
That part of her you hid from us
As we went on our rampage of destruction.

Guide me into the hidden groves
    Where the virgin trees
      Hang heavy with sweet fruits.
I will tell no one of its location;
For I will never leave—never go back.

I seek amnesty, oh merciful one.
Give me sanctuary.

I know that we are beyond
Even your understanding;
As we call for the ascension
Yet savor our own downfall—
    Beg for salvation
Yet revel in our own self-destruction.

Yet I do not ask this lightly.

I shall not seek to leave,
The moment after you bring me in.
I come unto you adamant and ardent.

You have allowed other souls to return home
    To the sanctuary you have preserved.
Now I ask you to bring me to that *Other Shore*.

You—whose eyes can look beyond flesh—
        Look into my heart
And tell me if I am not sincere in my declarations.
…Tell me if the changes I have made
    Are not more than skin-deep.

What offering may I bring as a show of my sincerity?
There is nothing you could possibly want
From this world we have built.

All things here give only the illusion of fulfillment
And I shall not dishonor you any further
By bringing you any such false gifts.

No…all I have to give you is myself—
    The years of my life to come,
    Which I will devote to you.

All I can offer are the sacred parts of myself:
    My heart, my lifetime,
    My body and my promise.

Tell me, is that enough
To cover the debt of what we have taken?

Most likely not; for we have taken *everything*.

Yet in your magnanimity
I know you will accept what I have
    And forgive the balance.

Being the person you are
You shall accept nothing from me;
    Instead you shall give all you have to me.
You shall swathe me in the softest robes of hand-spun cotton,
    Wrap around me long shawls of purest gauzy linen,
    Hand to me the overflowing cup of thy paternal love
    And set in front of me a plate of perfectly ripened fruits
                Picked by thine own hand.

You who we dishonored,
You who we defamed,
You who we defaced…
    You will embrace us
With no bitterness in your heart.

Tell me, how such an act of forgiveness is possible?
Do you love us that deeply?
And if so,
    How could we have ever chosen to leave you?

Showing the faith you still have in us
You are willing to invite us
Into the last refuge you have.

Rest easy wounded father,
    Fret not
Trembling mother,
I shall not harm a single leaf within this Elysium.
I shall not trample a single blade of grass
Or disturb in the slightest,
The deep calm which resonates here.

No, I shall walk in introspect
Through the blooming sanctum
Of this untouched place knowing that,
While I am a part of this greatness,
It is greater still.

I shall do no harm;
Instead I want only to be able
To give all that I am to it,
    That I might have the honor of adding
    To this gathering of all things ancient.

I shall ask for nothing;
Instead I want only to offer my life
    To the protection and preservation of this perfection.

L.M. Browning

L.M. Browning grew up in a small fishing village in Connecticut. A longtime student of religion, nature and philosophy these themes permeate her work. Browning is a award-winning author and wildlife artist. In 2010 she wrote a Pushcart Prize nominated contemplative poetry series: *Oak Wise, Ruminations at Twilight* and *The Barren Plain*. In late 2011 she celebrated the release of her first full-length novel: *The Nameless Man*. She is a graduate from the University of London and a Fellow with the League of Conservationist Writers. In 2010 she accepted a partnership at Hiraeth Press—an independent publisher of ecological titles. She is an Associate Editor of Written River: A Journal of Eco-Poetics as well as Founder and Executive Editor of The Wayfarer: A Journal of Contemplative Literature. In 2011 Browning opened Homebound Publications—an independent publisher of contemplative literature based in New England. Her latest book is, *Fleeting Moments of Fierce Clarity: Journal of a New England Poet*. For more information visit: www.lmbrowning.com

Foreword by J.K. McDowell

J.K. McDowell is an artist, poet and mystic, an Ohioan expat living in Cajun country. Always immersed in poetry, raised in Buckeye country by a mother who told of Sam I Am, Danny Deaver and Annabel Lee and a father who quoted Shakespeare and Omar Khayyam. In the last decade a deepened study of poetry and shamanism and nature has inspired a regular practice of writing poetry that blossomed into the works presented in this collection. Lately, mixing Lorca and Lovecraft, McDowell lives twenty miles north of the Gulf Coast with his soul mate who also happens to be his wife and their two beautiful companion parrots. He is the author of *Night, Mystery & Light* [Hiraeth Press 2011] Visit his poetry blog at: www.nightmysteryandlight.wordpress.com

HOMEBOUND
PUBLICATIONS
Independent Publisher of Contemplative Titles

GOING BACK TO GO FORWARD is the philosophy of Homebound. We recognize the importance of going home to gather from the stores of old wisdom to help nourish our lives in this modern era. We choose to lend voice to those individuals who endeavor to translate the old truths into new context. Our titles introduce insights concerning mankind's present internal, social and ecological dilemmas.

It is the intention of those at Homebound to revive contemplative storytelling. We publish introspective full-length novels, parables, essay collections, epic verse, short story collections, journals and travel writing. In our fiction titles our intention is to introduce a new mythology that will directly aid mankind in the trials we face at present.

The stories humanity lives by give both context and perspective to our lives. Some older stories, while well-known to the generations, no longer resonate with the heart of the modern man nor do they address the present situation we face individually and as a global village. Homebound chooses titles that balance a reverence for the old wisdom; while at the same time presenting new perspectives by which to live.

WWW.HOMEBOUNDPUBLICATIONS.COM

CPSIA information can be obtained at www.ICGtesting.com
Printed in the USA
BVOW05s1248090414

349930BV00003B/20/P